Resting
Stripper

Rocker girls,
North Circular Road
'We don't go out with a bloke that
didn't have a motor-bike.

LONDON A LA MODE

drawings and captions by
Paul Hogarth
text by
Malcolm Muggeridge

Hill and Wang · New York

Contents

'I turned my thoughts to a more novel mode, *viz.* drawing contemporary *mores*, a field not confined to country or age. I endeavoured to treat my subjects as a dramatist, my picture is my stage, and men and women my players, who by means of certain actions and gestures, are to exhibit a dumb show.'

Shakespeare, as quoted by William Hogarth in his Autobiography

Preface

My London is a complex jungle of nine million souls hell-bent on the good things of life. An empire has been and gone, and the offices of departed power dot the West End like carcases in a pasture of skyscrapers. To the East, the great warehouses line a Thames blackened with bygone filth. Once they were filled with gold and silks from India, sugar from the West Indies, timber and tobacco from North America. Now, they are stuffed with detergents and pet-foods, and other necessities of a thriving consumer economy.

The idle and the industrious are with us as the industriously idle and the idly industrious. It is sometimes difficult to tell which is which. There are so many more of us now. Leisure from automation has created a boredom which for so many of us can only be dispelled by the constant pursuit of pleasure. And why not? So, London of the 1960s has revived for all, and in good measure, the riotous gaiety and pungent contrasts of the 1760s. Only more so. Not only do we have good food, stylish clothes, vice and gambling but our very own pop, striptease for everyman and organized crime.

How can any artist interested in his time ignore such subject matter? The unbridled vitality of the days and nights of our capital city is the envy of the civilized world. It is a paradise for our questing pencils!

Paul HOGARTH

Morning

On the bald street breaks the blank day

I first consciously set eyes on London seated beside my father in what must have been one of the very last hansom cabs to ply for hire along Moorgate. The first time I was aware of it as a distinctive place was from the top of a motor-bus on Armistice Day, November 11, 1918, when I observed with wonder and some alarm crowds surging through the streets and into the parks to couple under the trees. Subsequently, I passed much of my life there, both in terms of time and of expense of spirit; questing for money, women, fame, all inferior satisfactions. It has been an intimacy more of hate than love; but still an intimacy, giving me the feeling that the place in its squalid way is eternal. London Bridge, after all, still has not fallen down despite T. S. Eliot, Hitler, and those innumerable feet which pound across it each morning and evening. If a million years were to pass, and I then to hear St Paul's clock chime, catch a whiff of floral scent against the Covent Garden stench of rotting vegetables, breathe into my nostrils the dank, dark flow of Thames, I should know instantly where I was – in London.

I stay when in London in a small room near the Inner Temple. There are newspaper offices all around, in most of which I have worked in my time. My feet have so often trodden the pavements in this part of London. The alleyways and bars and obscure corners are all known to me, and the very smell – compounded of printer's ink, frying fat, bad breath and beer spillings – is permanently in my nostrils.

The nearness to these old haunts makes me more than usually restless in spirit. Through the night I rise and fall with the successive editions as they come off the rotary presses, rushing to and from the stone, poring over damp galleys, yelling, stampeding, and then relaxing to gather strength and energy for the next bout. My heart and the presses beat together, and I suppose always will. Through my sleep I hear the coloured vans make off, furiously starting up and accelerating as they carry away the next day's paper, to be pushed through letter-boxes, laid beside milk bottles, sold to somnambulistic commuters, and then laid aside to wrap fish or stop broken windows. I have spent so much of my time attuned to this rhythm that it abides with me, as, back on land after a sea voyage, one still seems to be afloat.

From my window I can see the dawn break round St Paul's, whose dark dome floats mysteriously in the brightening sky. I

The 740 to Liverpool St
from Cambridge

9

LIVERPOOL STREET A.M.

make tea – that insomniac's brew – sucking down cup after cup as I gaze balefully at the day's beginnings, and survey with vague distaste what it holds: the encounters and telephone calls, the business and desires – such as they are. Dawn is a time for thoughts of death and of God. The silence and coolness, the fragility, make the world seem easily forsaken. A time to slip away – 'Dearest, I didn't like to wake you.'

I, too, love the dawn, and remember past dawns like love affairs – lurid across the yellow desert, a mounting glow out of the Mediterranean, palely lighting up Arctic wastes, spreading like a deep blush over leaden tropical skies. Leaning out of the window I look down on the empty littered street below. Soon it will fill with tramping feet, bobbing heads, hurrying bodies. Across the way cleaners are moving from room to room, emptying the

London markets are a swearing uproar in the early light of dawn. Billingsgate has the wit. Cockle and winkle men up from Lambeth and Stepney are greeted with, 'Do yer flies up mates, you'll catch cold!'

Early morning traffic over Tower Bridge

Tower Bridge

waste-paper baskets ready for them to be filled again, removing cigarette ends and milk bottles, dusting down the desks. Already the first arrivals for the evening papers are beginning to appear, their seats still warm from the morning ones' last departures. Nothing en s, nothing begins. London is eternity – of a sort.

Soon I venture into the street myself, tingling with after-shave lotion, washed and dusted and brushed, peppermint tooth-paste tasting in my mouth. Down on the Embankment the rush has already begun: cars roaring past, momentarily held up at traffic signals, like wild animals on a leash, then off again faster than ever; pedestrians moving briskly along with resolute, purposive steps, girls tap-tapping as their stiletto heels hit the asphalt, men remote inside bowler hats, umbrellas swinging on their arms, brief-cases clutched. They move concertedly, like a flight of bees or a procession of ants, yet each one is wrapped up in a particular purpose, has a particular destination. Each is the centre of his own universe. Together they are solitary, as in solitude they are together.

An occasional pair are holding hands or arms, or even clasped together. Is it, I ask myself, a dawn pick-up, love at sunrise? Some romance of the Southern Electric, born in packed carriages, eight a side and five down the middle? A love consummated in jammed corridors, where the lovers are pushed remorselessly against one another, breast to breast? As the wheels rumble past Croydon East, what blissful stirrings of the flesh! Hurtling through New Cross, what joy in one another's arms! Can it be London Bridge already? – the nightingale, surely, not the lark!

Take a generous mixture of people in round black hats, carrying identical briefcases and rolled umbrellas. Pack tightly into battered old trains. Move steadily in direction of Baker Street, Cannon Street, Charing Cross, Waterloo and Liverpool Street. Play 'Colonel Bogey' on tape as soon as doors open. Divert mixture downwards into maw of warm Underground, mix freely and serve up in all shops and offices.

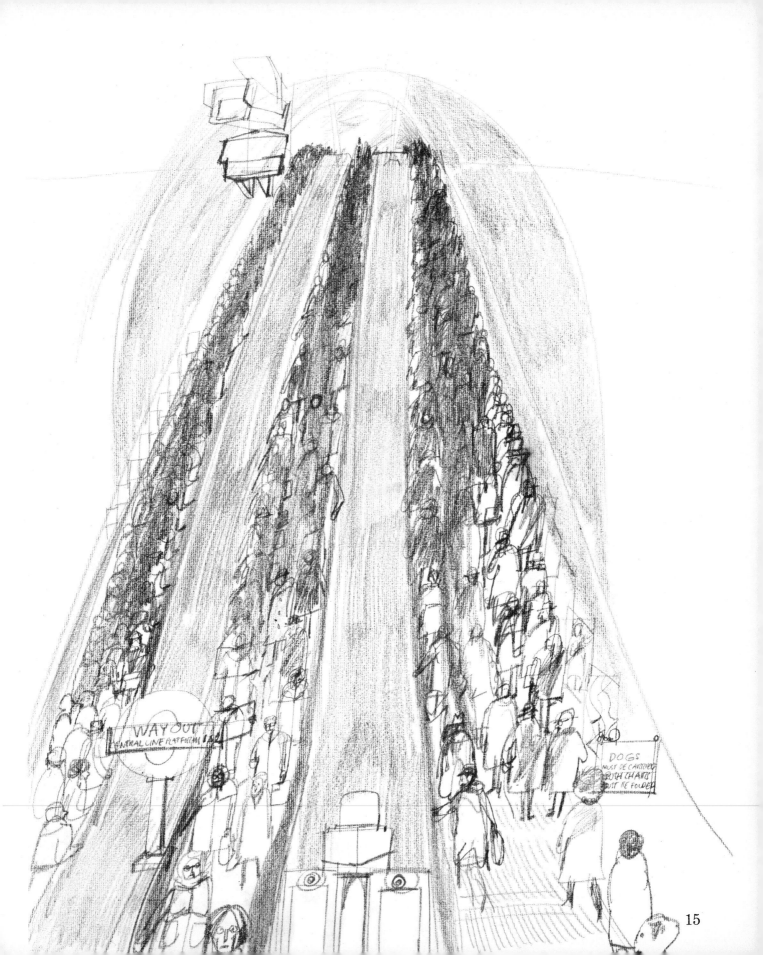

15

Good Morning.
This is London Airport asking all foreigners to put out their ghastly cigarettes and speak English.
Thank you.

To the west of Battersea Park, there is a great grinding of gears and squealing of brakes. And across the Albert Bridge there is a great traffic jam.

Moving with the others, my anxieties diminish. The floating dome of St Paul's increased them, picking out my ego like a spotlight to shrink and shiver in the glare. Now striding purposively from nowhere to nowhere, I am serene. Momentarily, I have attained the quest of mid-twentieth-century man, and lost my separate identity. These great cities with their sprouting aerials for dreaming spires, with their crowded streets and everlasting movement, meet an essential requirement of our time. London is an enormous vat, steaming and bubbling, into which egos can be thrown to make a single scalding brew.

Just before reaching the Savoy (coffee fumes rising, toast crisping, and already in the grill-room preparations being made for the expense-account men, who will soon come ravening in, cigar-cured, and flakes of smoked salmon about their mouths) I branch off with the tributary flowing through Embankment

17

I went to the Houses of Parliament, full of hope and excitement for an interesting morning. Big Ben chimes nine and I've just finished my outside impression.

It's time to collect my permit to draw inside. I am given the paper, but told I 'can't draw now, the Members are showing parties of their constituents round.' I am advised to go and have coffee downstairs until the House sits at 11 o'clock. I make my way importantly downstairs but a stalwart constable bars my path: 'Can't go down there, sir, without permission.' Feeling like Joyce Cary's immortal Gulley Jimson,

I retrace my steps, and take revenge by making a fast sketch behind a motionless crocodile of Scots schoolgirls. A clock chimes eleven, so I ascend to the Strangers' Gallery. I have a wonderful view of the representatives of the people. I am about to draw, my pencil at the ready, when I read that 'Strangers are not permitted to read books or papers, draw or write, stand in or behind galleries, or carry opera glasses or cameras.' A custodian gazes at me steadily. As I leave, I am invited to return and draw during the summer recess. 'There'll be nobody here at all then, sir.'

Gardens. On we go, past the flower-beds, arranged like troops, and the benches on which an occasional sleeper, unshaved, mouth open, with the ineffably sad look of sleeping men, remains undisturbed by our passage; past the statues – a bearded Robert Raikes, founder of Sunday Schools (I saw him on a morning in the Blitz with one of his metal arms blown off, his dignity unimpaired), a mountainous Burns; past the deck-chairs where already one or two recline, sucking in the thin morning sunshine through hungry mouths. (Ah, the lust of the godless for sun! – mopping it up like a gourmet wiping his plate with bread.) Then out into Villiers Street, where Kipling once lodged, in his early twenties and just home from India. I imagine him peering sycophantically through thick spectacle lenses at towering troopers in red with whores on their arms.

Early morning in Trafalgar Square

Mid-morning in the City.
In the Stock Exchange, brokers and jobbers grimace with well-timed enthusiasm,
which makes this old-established institution the envy of the civilized world.

Mid-morning in Mayfair.
At Sotheby's, New Bond Street,
the contents of yet another stately home
are swiftly auctioned off by the unctuously skilful hammer-men.

22

84-year-old Jeanne de Gebsattel, a Luxembourg baroness, once had a big place herself. A Londoner by adoption, she now lives in a tiny flat in Hampstead. 'In my day,' she began, 'rich people (aristocrats, that is) did not take jobs. Now, they take what they can get.' The Baroness has been a char, busker, cook and night nurse. Now a model, she sits for art students at the Slade, the Royal College of Art and St. Martin's. She also swims. Since she came to England in 1934 she has been a regular at Highgate Ponds, summer and winter. 'I arrived in London just before Christmas and knew nothing about the Boxing Day Swim in the Serpentine. That year,' she went on, 'the ice was not broken enough to hold the race but I saw a patch of open water and jumped in!'

Baroness de Gebsattel

23

This is Bow Street Police Station. Here, opposite the Royal Opera House, Covent Garden, can be seen as varied a bunch of characters as any to be found in the novels of our great Charles Dickens. A strumpet shrills defiance; the too well-loved son is wept over by his handsome mother; a motorist, chastened by a savage fine, makes for the solace of a drinking club.

right A glimpse into the World of the Other Half. The first morning of the Annual Men's Sale at Harrod's.

The street markets of the East End thrive anew in the Affluent 'Sixties. Petticoat Lane, Whitechapel; a market since the sixteenth century. Sells anything from socks to sausage with Mediterranean exuberance. *Playboy* has taken the place of the shifty man with plain envelopes, but handsome Indians still stride through the Lane with bunches of silk scarves.

Club Row, Bethnal Green.
Side by side with gummy-eyed kittens and mongrels of doubtful origin,
fondled by the wide boys, are some handsome specimens.
There are singing birds and racing pigeons, too.

The new buildings soar everywhere,
and London's only example of Elizabethan Domestic,
in High Holborn, looks like Noah's Ark.

28

LEICESTER SQUARE

Good old Leicester Square, where William Hogarth grew up.
Once a favourite spot for duellists.
Now famous for its morons, pornographic bookshops and chicken dinners.

London's only *art nouveau* garage,
the Michelin service station on the corner
of Brompton Road and Sloane Avenue.

Trafalgar Square, heart of the
Commonwealth, and one of
the finest sites in Europe for
pigeons, pick-ups and street
photographers.

With the dogs of Chelsea.
The morning walk, Anderson Street, off the King's Road.

The morning walk, Royal Avenue.
In the distance is the Chelsea Hospital, pad of all Chelsea Pensioners.

33

King Alfred held court in Chelsea, but now it's the turn of the Chelsea Pensioners. They plod around the streets, sample the odd pint of ale, pose for art students and chat up the last of the nannies. They are a *corps d'élite* of veterans who, in the words of the old song, 'never die but simply fade away'. They come in two sorts — disability and long service. All have to be at least sixty years old and to have served in the Regular Army. Men of this age are called 'sonnies' and only graduate as 'real men' at seventy-five.

Chelsea pensioners are long-lived. Yorkie, on the left, is eighty.

Said he: 'We don't lose many before ninety!' He joined Kitchener's New Army in 1915. 'I need yer, the poster sed, so I went.'

Moustached Andy Smedley behind is a 'sonnie' at sixty. Served twenty-one years in the Grenadier Guards and another twenty in the Royal Artillery.

Pensioners
in parade dress

Paul HOGARTH: CHELSEA PENSIONERS

I made several flying visits to
London as a boy, with Mum and
Dad. There were arguments and
aching feet; it was always hot.
I remember the Lyons' teashops
and the Cumberland Hotel, but
most of all the Changing of the
Guard at Buckingham Palace.
When I returned to draw them,
the guardsmen looked smaller,
more vulnerable, but the people
who watch haven't changed a bit.

The Dell
HydePIC

Not many left of the Old Guard
nannies either. At the traditional
rendezvous, The Dell, Hyde Park,
a new generation takes over.

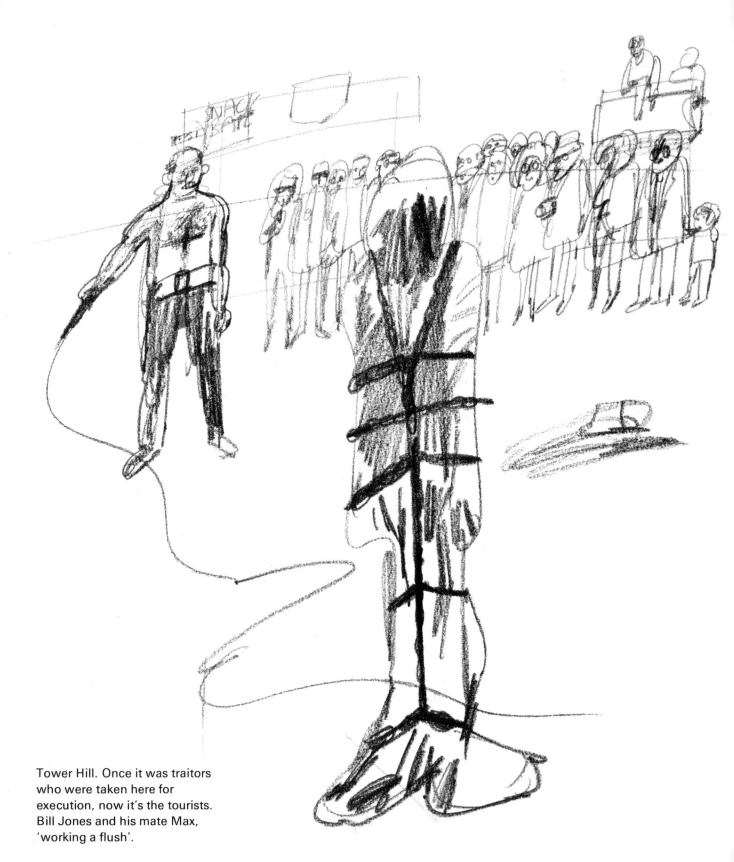

Tower Hill. Once it was traitors
who were taken here for
execution, now it's the tourists.
Bill Jones and his mate Max,
'working a flush'.

38

At Speakers' Corner, Hyde Park.
A Sunday morning show with a
medley cast of exhibitionists and
buskers, playing for the pennies of
the lonely and bored.

'Tattoed Jack' (Jacobus Van Dyn)
looks on. A voice is heard asking
him why he had his face tattoed.
'I wos born like this,' he replies.
'Me mum was a tattoed lidy. Bless
you ma'am, best of luck!' (Aside)
'I wish those bleedin' coppers wud
piss orf.' Speakers' Corner is
part of the Queen's Property, and
collection of money is illegal.

Dan Forbes, thirty-five years at the Corner,
always brings his glasses to get a close look at the action.

'You can't *buy* love, my friends . . .'
Voice: 'Yer too right matie, too
bloody dear *these* days!'

43

Noon

How London doth pour out her citizens!

At Charing Cross Station commuters come pouring out from every exit, swelling the onward rush along the Strand, towards the Law Courts, Chancery Lane, Fleet Street, Ludgate Circus and the City: an enormous human tidal wave which daily washes into London in the morning and out again in the evening. Battling now against the stream instead of going with it, I push and shove my way into the Station. ('Never forget,' a Stranger said to me once in the lobby of the Midland Hotel in Manchester, 'that only dead fish swim with the stream.' 'Yes, Brother,' I wanted to reply as we shook hands, 'but dead fish swim quietly.')

At the news-stand I charge myself with the morning papers. What a precious load! Triumphantly I bear it away to one of Mr Forte's cafés across the road. There, perched on a high stool, lapped in muzak – sounds and sweet airs which give delight and hurt not, as on Caliban's Island – I am served with orange juice, coffee and toast by a majestic Negro waitress, her flesh velvet-black against the white of her overall, her mouth a red cavern, her hair piled darkness.

Eating and swallowing, trance-like I absorb the news. For me it is a fix; peace and oblivion descend as the headlines get into my blood-stream. The gossip paragraphs nestle round my heart, and the small type hangs in clouds about my head like tobacco smoke – 'Grave News From Laos', ' "No More Bloody-Mindedness" Says P.M.', 'Road Deaths Reach New Peak', 'Rumpus At U.N.', 'Earl's Son To Marry'. The printed words and pictures obliterate their own sense; why, having read, I am a man again. What's Laos to me now? Let blood spatter the tarmac and earl's sons marry as they please – what care I? They ever must believe a lie who see with, not through, the eye, Blake wrote, prophetically envisaging us, whose lens-eyes reflect such sparkling and such varied lies, all ever to be believed.

Tranquillised, I climb down from my stool, bow to the waitress and make off, leaving my crumpled newspapers behind me, like empty capsules whose precious contents have been sucked into a hypodermic. Outside, the Strand is quieter now, all those hurrying commuters scattered into their burrows and out of sight; even the traffic less impetuous. Already the first evening paper bills are on display – 'Famous Singer Dead'. What singer? How famous? Reputations burgeon at this hour. Even I, I reflect, dying at such a time might have my brief moment. 'Famous Writer

Mooney's in the Strand 12

Dies'? – no, I fear not. 'Well-known Journalist Dies'? – just possible, for the dog-racing edition only. 'Death of TV Man'? – the most likely, always assuming that no better choice, like an M.P. or former gaiety girl, presents itself. From frame to frame, oh, flickering image, where lies thy sting?

From Trafalgar Square I turn into St James's Park, as I so often have. Parks are for the likes of me. How many hours I've mooned away in them, how many miles I've tramped across them! – Green Park, Hyde Park, Regent's Park, Hampstead Heath; sad thoughts by the Serpentine, rendez-vous by the tall tulips, quarrelling among the roses, reconciliation within sight of the Mappin Terraces, within sound of the petulant roar of lions in cages. Since there's no help, come let us kiss and part.

An occasional senior civil servant, a Principal or perhaps Under-Secretary, even at this hour is walking, his hat in his hand, through St James's Park in the direction of Whitehall and his in-tray. Otherwise there are only children and their nursemaids, the elderly and indifferent like myself, to enjoy the green grass underfoot, the sparkling ornamental water and the bustling birds. Deck

'El Vino's'. Here, in this modest heart of Fleet Street, can be seen some of its biggest backsides.

At one time, the poor and ambitious were as welcome under the well-nourished girl caryatids of the Café Royal as the rich and successful. Now all is affluence unbridled in the fairyland of the Grill Room. 'His tastes were modest,' wrote Will Rothenstein of his friend, Max Beerbohm, 'Hansom cabs, telegrams and coffee at the Café Royal.' I doubt whether the incomparable Max would get away with just that these days. He might.

chairs, two by two, are placed in position under the trees, but from the evening before – dead souls now – and there are cigarette ends and ice-cream wrappings round the band-stand. I linger for a while, and then cross Horse Guards Parade, pushing through the little crowd assembled for the changing of the guard. Cameras hang over their breasts like a third eye. Without its confirmation who would ever believe what their eyes have seen? Would they even believe it themselves?

On an impulse I hail a taxi, and then, when it stops, realise that I must tell the driver where to go. Where am I going? And, by the way, is it yesterday, tomorrow or today? Taxi-drivers are viewers; I am recognised, and dare not pretend I'm someone else – which, in point of fact, I might well be. Status demands that I should be going somewhere urgently. 'El Vino,' I say sternly, 'and as quickly as you can. I'm late for an appointment.' Ominously,

Noon in the Punch Tavern
Fleet Street

Noon in peaceful
'Punch Tavern,' Fleet Street

the driver opens the glass partition between us for conversation. He was very interested, he says, in my conversation the other evening with Lady Churchill. Mrs Roosevelt, I correct him and she's dead, adding to myself: 'And so am I.' He brushes the correction aside as an irrelevance. Mrs Roosevelt, dead or alive, or Lady Churchill – what's the difference? As we drive along, darting dangerously through the traffic to keep my non-appointment, the driver animadverts with great emphasis, and even some indignation, on my non-conversation with a pseudo person.

In the chromium elegance of Prunier's, time appears to have little significance. The world of Sartre's *Huis Clos*, of life aboard some obscure avant-garde liner of yesteryear, are brought to mind, as all wage a sustained offensive on the formidable menu.

An ever-jostling throng of irrepressible Britons makes Piccadilly the bustling hub of the capital.

Meanwhile, lucky showgirls are being taken for lunch at the Ivy.

This is Regent's Canal, or 'Little Venice', as it is sometimes called. 'Watch out for the bridge, ladies and gentlemen. Little boys sometimes do the unmentionable!'

53

Stages of Cruelty: Scene One The Monkey House. Bunteresque schoolboys shower baboons with peanut shells. Schoolgirls titter at colourful exposures. Gargantuan mums giggle uncontrollably.

Stages of Cruelty: Scene Two
But who is being cruel to who?

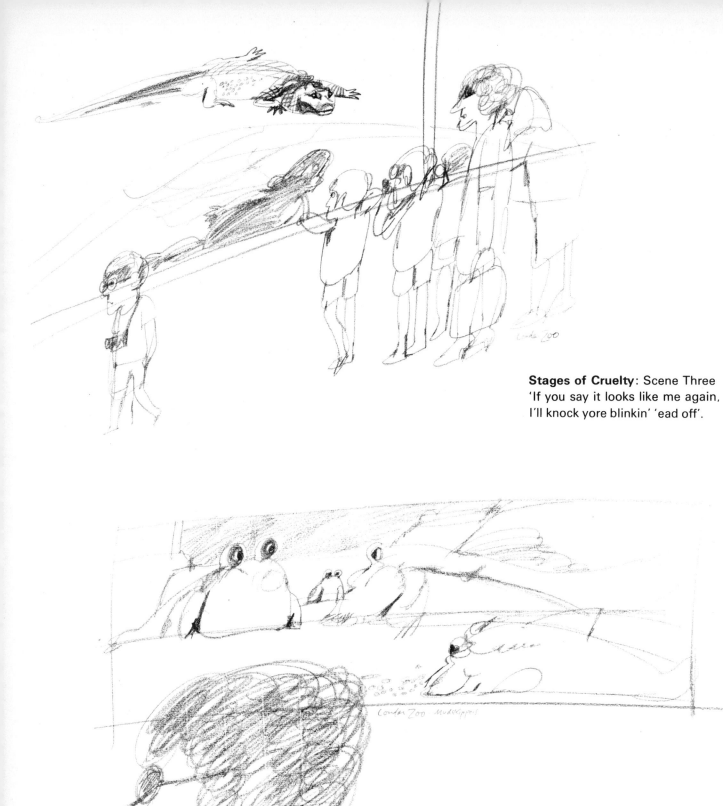

Stages of Cruelty: Scene Three
'If you say it looks like me again,
I'll knock yore blinkin' 'ead off'.

Stages of Cruelty: Scene Four
In the Aquarium;
Mudskippers discuss a viewer.

At Madame Tussaud's.
In the Hall of Mirrors, fun-lovers
are soon initiated into the
atmosphere of unquiet aimlessness.

The causes which embittered
Madame Tussaud against humanity
have never been satisfactorily
explained. It must have been no
common injury which prompted her
to take this terrible revenge.

In the Chamber of Horrors, open-mouthed courting couples and questing Irish girls giggle helplessly. Boys boggle. Middle-aged women are 'sent' by scowling, handsome Victorian bluebeards.

Myself, I like the War Museum down in Lambeth, and most of all in the afternoon. Its interior houses a vast jumble of memorabilia from both World Wars. Sopwith Camels and DH5's swing on high above thickets of machine-guns. Wide-eyed German teenagers chatter gutturally before battlefield diaromas. Grandads wander among snipers in glass cases. An attendant looms above me: 'They all comes 'ere, sir: egg-'eads, grey-'eads, square-'eads and rockers. Wot abahrt a good fillum? Starts in five minutes. *The Fields of Sacrifice* in technycolour!'

Kinky!

Opening Day, Chelsea Flower Show.
'I don't like begonias, much,
but my god these are beautiful m'dear!'

'Mummy insisted that we come,
and here we are. A frightful bore
really but you never know who you
might meet.'

CHELSEA
FLOWER SHOW

Gerd Siemoneits wild animals.

The old timers say that circuses just aren't wot they used to be. Grock, Pimpo and Dannie Leno, they were the masters. The really great days have gone for ever. But the show-men of the Bertram Mills Circus (traditionally performed over Christmas and New Year at Olympia) try hard enough to dazzle the young and satisfy the sensation-seeking.

A glittering cavalcade introduce us to acts from the Big Tops of many nations. The Gordons, who use bull-whips, kick off the bill proper; they're from Czechoslovakia. At a spanking pace follow Belgian sea-lions, Russian clowns, Portuguese jugglers, Italian pigeons, French footballing dogs, Danish horses, Dutch chimpanzee acrobats and British elephants.

The Germans open the second half with a mixed wild animal dance ensemble. Cycling South Africans follow a death-defying American high-wire act, and finally there's a triple-somersaulting Mexican flying trapeze show. More than anyone expects to see at any man's circus, in fact.

Teddy Coronis sealions

Olympia is a great place for exhibitions.
After the circus I look in on the Racing Car Show.
Here, *aficionados* of all ages gaze at Jim Clark's Lotus,
in which he won the 1965 Indianapolis '500'.

It's gone two o'clock.
Over in Soho, the strip clubs and
gambling parlours are open for business.

A sunny June day dawns, and families hump hold-alls over Epsom Downs. Quiet refreshment is readily available in big cosy tents.

Then, what looks like the spearhead of a mass evacuation of all London approaches on the horizon. People everywhere.

By noon the Downs are a struggling, heaving jumble of buses, trucks, cars, motor-bikes, scooters and bicycles. It is Derby Day.

'Never seen folks eat like they do 'ere.'

'You'd think they'd turn it up on a day like this, wouldn't yer? Not on your nellie! Wouldn't be the same without 'em though.'

A quiet nosh of jellied eels between races

The home stretch

Derby Day: in the Paddock

The Sport of nobs . . . and of gypsies

Derby Day: Gypsies

Placing bets

Toy sellers

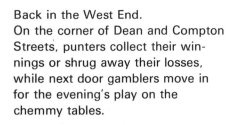

Back in the West End.
On the corner of Dean and Compton
Streets, punters collect their win-
nings or shrug away their losses,
while next door gamblers move in
for the evening's play on the
chemmy tables.

78

In the gardens of Soho Square,
I watch gentle old Frenchwomen
converse with frail Viennese, and
listen to Italian women insult
their employers.

79

Carnaby Street, Soho.
Joe Zurbini, who once owned a
'caf' in 'the Carnaby' five short
years ago, reminisced as he
watched me drawing. 'Full of pubs
at one time,' he said, 'fourteen
of 'em. Now the kids are blueing it
on clobber.' Saturday afternoon is
clobber time. The Mods ('call us
stylists') come in from all over
town, on foot and in sports cars,
to look at the newest gear. The
boutiques are sprung like traps,
each with its record-player.

81

Evening

Faint struggles with the tedium of time

The bar is still almost empty. I sit in a corner by myself watching it fill. The same rubicund faces and loud, assertive voices as of old; the same disguised sycophancy – laughing at a joke a shade too loudly and long, attention a shade too ostentatious. (Were they the same faces? Or just similar ones? I am not quite sure.) So many happenings that I associate with this place – the Abdication, Munich, Suez. Voices vociferously raised, growing thicker as the glasses empty; tables banged. We knew about it all, the inside story. Then, footsteps perhaps a little unsteady, back to our type-writers, the keyboard letters displaying an alarming tendency to run together. Never mind, from long practice we can manage – writing almost automatic by now; words shaping themselves and dissolving on their own, without the help of any outside mind or fingers.

I note among the bar's frequenters that wary expression so characteristic of their trade; that straining of the ears and search-ing of the eyes, and out of habit find myself falling into the same way, until I remember that I need no longer have any concern about what that man's heard or the other knows. After all, the faces are *not* the same. I am among strangers. Getting up to go, one or two, as I observe, nudge each other, looking pointedly in my direction as though to say: 'I wonder what he's doing here.' I, too, wonder.

It is time to eat again. Meals divide the London day, which otherwise would be just one unbroken, featureless succession of hours. Breakfast, lunch, tea, dinner, supper – these are the fixed points round which the day revolves, as, elsewhere, it might be dawn, high-noon, evening and nightfall. The duty to eat is one of the few remaining ones. I eat, therefore I am.

For the solitary outsider like myself, the question is: Where? I survey the various possibilities. A club? – that hum of over-ripe voices; those too, too solid marble busts and gilded picture frames; dark suits and polished shoes drifting into the dining-room like cows trooping into a meadow of lush buttercup pasture; the clatter of cutlery and the hum of talk, the padding waiters bearing warmed-up sole, the ghosts of past meals and the phantoms of meals to come which hover through the tainted air. No, not a club.

What about a familiar restaurant? 'Alone today, sir?' Not a hint of consternation, or even surprise, as the head waiter beckons me to a place to sit and munch in by myself, amidst the boisterous

City of Westminster
ST. MARTINS GV
WC2

NORTHERN LINE — LEICESTER SQ STATION

6 pm.

parties, the couples gazing avidly into each other's eyes. Immaculate in black coat and striped trousers, he glides silently, unerringly, adjusting his manner to his instinctive sense of his clients' fortunes. He is a barometer, and I, being alone, send the mercury down.

Alternatively, a strange restaurant? There the head waiter, eyeing me coldly, murmurs: 'A place for one!' Then a start of recognition. On my own! How's that? Something must have gone wrong. Thus television, like an absent tyrant, exerts its domination even when one is well out of range of the cameras. One belongs to the cameras, and has no separate existence apart from them. One is their creature. They control one's going out and one's coming in. Before the start of recognition in the eyes of strangers one insensibly falls into one's allotted role, reading allotted lines off the autocue to the accompaniment of the studio audience's allotted cheers. To be known is not to exist; to be known universally would be to be obliterated wholly.

The best escape from the domination of the cameras is to, as it

were, jump out of the screen and join the viewers, who only see what they expect to see. Among them, I am unknown. In a self-service café I pick up my tray and walk, looking in at the various dishes arranged each in its own neon-lit glass cubicle, and choosing here a roll, there a pat of butter, there cheese and an apple; all these frozen, chromium-flavoured delicacies washed down with a glass of frozen milk. Thus I am fed.

By the Law Courts anxious litigants are waiting, florid men in wigs walking self-importantly among them. I vaguely recognise a judge. What a shabby, dingy little man in his crumpled suit and absurd wing-collar, with rheumy eyes and a large, fleshy nose! I imagine him in court robed in red and ermine. How impressive he then becomes! Where would our earthly justice be without such trappings? Undress the judge, and Law itself stands revealed in all its fraudulence and inadequacy.

So reflecting, I turn into Lincoln's Inn Fields where the sunshine has brought out typists in large numbers to munch biscuits and drink from cardboard cups. A man on a folding platform is proclaiming the end of the world to a policeman who seems to be his only audience. I join the policeman. London, the man says, is doomed; its destruction is at hand. We should all take heed and repent. He might well be right. 'Hear! hear!' I ejaculate. It does not please him. He frowns, suspecting, perhaps, that I am mocking him; or maybe he prefers to be a lone voice. The typists, in any case, munch on regardless of their City's fate. In due course the man folds up his platform, shoulders it, and makes off presumably to set it up elsewhere.

The afternoon wears on. Too late now to make for High Holborn where I am expected. I eye apprehensively three telephone booths, little confessionals side by side, and decide not to breathe their foetid air. As for the cocktail party to meet Mr Henry Luce – Oh, Life, oh Time, oh Fortune, I am unworthy. There is nothing to do but wait for night to fall. In London, I reflect, everyone is always waiting – for trains to come in or to go out, for posts to be collected or delivered, for the first customer to present himself and the last to go. Always waiting, until at last one realises there is nothing to wait for; the rendez-vous will never be kept, and the inexorable parting never take place. Still I wait on, and the shadows lengthen, the light fades; the sounds of footsteps, cars and striking clocks are muffled. All those who emerged from Charing Cross in the morning now make their way thither. The human tidal wave is in reverse; another day has passed, another night has come.

Good Evening.
I am drawing in Pall Mall, with the distinct impression that everyone just isn't interested in what I am doing.

Blackfriars Bridge.
Most go home, right on home, to famil

VICTORIA R.
1896

Blackfriars Bridge

In summer, some go up to Alexandra
Park for an evening's flat racing.
At this punter-mecca the very
youngest and the very oldest horses
run; and the slaty old lavs are
covered with bitter legends.
'Bookies,' gouged Morrie Levi,' are
the lowest form of animal life.'

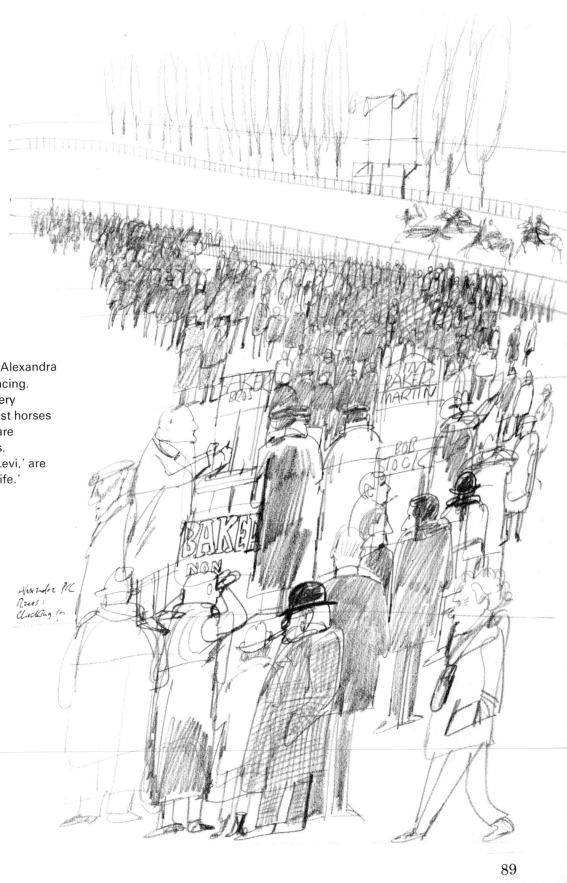

But most switch on the telly . . .

For the first time since early morning, the streets of Soho are empty. If they haven't gone home to watch the telly, they are having a quiet one to start the evening.

Opening time at the 'Salisbury', St Martin's Lane.
This is an actors' and writers' pub on the main circuit.

My name is Paul Potts, occupation poet. I have just been drawn in my favourite haunt, the *York Minster*, in Dean Street, known to intimates as the 'French Pub'. I am having my first pint of the evening. I have asked Hogarth to make it clear that the photos behind me have nothing to do with the kind of life I lead.

Opening time at the 'Chelsea Potter', on the King's Road.

At 'Chez Victor',
a young General de Gaulle looks
benignly on what would pass for a
Left Bank restaurant.

The big Bingo halls are filling up, like this one, the ABC Commodore, Hammersmith.
Old and young are caught up in a dream-world of great expectations.

96

In the bowling-lanes, a relaxed atmosphere prevails. They are the new social centres of genial squares of all ages. At the Excel Lanes, Shaftesbury Avenue, the balls start rolling at 5 o'clock, but the busiest time is between seven and eight, and they keep on rolling until dawn. Postmen, printers, clerks and computer operators play each other in teams under names like *The Misfits, The Bookworms, The Dragons* and *The Who.* 'Wosn't allus like this, all 'appy like,' an attendant told me. 'Used to get Rockers and blokes wontin' a cheap kip for the night.'

At the Dogs, White City.

In Soho's intimate rooms,
public pleasures.

In and around the West End,
the chain of small Victorian and Edwardian theatres is opening.
The car parks fill up again.

This is the Aldwych Theatre,
off the Strand, the base of Peter Hall's
Royal Shakespeare Theatre Company.

The Palace Theatre, corner of
Shaftesbury Avenue and Charing
Cross Road.

Night

I wander thro' each charter'd street,
Near where the charter'd Thames does flow,
And mark in every face I meet
Marks of weakness, marks of woe.

Now the commuters have all gone home, packed tight for the return journey as they were for the journey up in the morning; trainload after trainload of them rumbling over the Thames. Suddenly the City is deserted, the Bank cavernous and empty, Threadneedle Street echoing with occasional footsteps; Cannon Street Station, shortly before filled to overflowing with a jostling multitude, now like an auditorium when the play is over and the audience have all departed; St Paul's, when I put my head in, likewise seems desolate and abandoned, with only a solitary verger in a black gown going his rounds, locking doors and extinguishing lights. I am alone under the dome.

All the life of London has shifted to the West. The day was for work, the night is for pleasure. Westwards, look! the lights are bright! Leicester Square is all ablaze, queues forming outside the cinemas, like souls gathering for admission to paradise; taxis creep and jerk along, and in restaurants the cutlery and seats, in constant use, never get a chance to cool – passed on warm from customer to customer. Through plate-glass windows I see them, neon-green, picking at their food like battery birds.

In spirit, I join in. We are pursuers of happiness, on the move – *nous passerons*; a mighty army marching as to joy – round Piccadilly Circus, along Coventry Street, and on to Charing Cross Road and Cambridge Circus. Our hopes and desires are written up in coloured lights, presented on screens in movement and colour; enlarged into a close-up of a body, a face, a magnified morsel of delectable flesh. All our appetites catered for – food whose succulent smell, warm and rich, assails us like a sirocco wind; drink borne on the breath of passers-by, and glimpsed through doors suddenly opened to reveal a shining bar within. Above all, sex, enfolding us, falling like black atomic rain on the just and unjust alike, rising from within and glowing without; an omnipresent radiance.

At the all-night chemist's all requisite aids to health and happiness are available – cosmetics for sweetening the flesh, hiding its blemishes, muffling its stenches; contraceptives to ensure that joy shall be unconfined, *sans peur et sans reproche*, not *virgo* but for ever *intacta*. Then the coloured pills, yellow, red and blue, green and white samite, mystic wonderful – pills for all purposes, to pep up and bank down, to send to sleep and awaken, to fatten and to reduce, to live and to die – that is, sleep for ever. 'Come unto me all ye that travail and are heavy-laden, and I will refresh you' – it is the druggist speaking. In his long white coat, benign behind his spectacles, he watches through the night, handing out his goodies, and never without recipients for them, including an occasional shivering junkie, who presents his prescription, and waits tremulously for his permitted allowance of capsules or tablets. Often when he gets them he doses himself then and there, not wishing to delay even for a little while the fulfilment of *his* happiness.

From Shaftesbury Avenue I move into Wardour Street, Frith Street, Old Compton Street, Greek Street and their little connecting lanes and alleys. Soho is warming up. Its afternoon visitors are for the most part old and timid – patrons of porno-films who sit by themselves in belted raincoats, their white heads bowed; or furtively explore the inner sanctums of porno-book shops, and watch dingy striptease shows with grave faces, like mourners at an Abbey funeral.

These have now all gone, or died. By night a younger, fresher clientele roams the streets. Whores have shaken off their torpor; make vigorously obscene gestures in doorways, peep alluringly out of windows; even venturesomely resume their old unmistakable walk, which can seem to be loitering or hurrying according to the eye of the beholder. Pimps whisper to passers-by of fleshly delicacies and oddities open to inspection. In the discotheques the young, tight-trousered and expressionless, take up their frozen

stances in a din of sound; in the strip-tease joints the middle-aged and elderly feast their eyes on the female form divine as it is slowly and tantalisingly unveiled to them, howling like desert hyenas as the last tiny wisp of cloth covering the last tiny bodily privacy is reached.

Sex is the commodity offered for edification and for sale; sex in the air breathed, sex the happiness pursued. Hungry eyes look round, and hungry flesh craves satisfaction. Sex stirs in each individual body, old and young, and hangs over all like a storm-cloud – vast lips meeting in suction across the sky, and giant bodies in copulation filling the universe. I think of St Paul's, huge, cavernous, empty. Here in these teeming, lighted, noisy Soho streets the religious mysteries of our time are celebrated. This is my body; do this in remembrance of me. In the beginning was the flesh, and the flesh was made Word. Except ye die in the spirit and are re-born in the flesh . . . Thus the New Testament is re-written.

Our heaven is earth, and London is its capital. London growing ever larger, sprawling ever further – street upon street upon street; many mansions, mansions of chromium and glass, rising ever higher into the sky; drawing to itself people, wealth, talent; motorways in and out, ever more cars, going ever faster. London! As the night wears on the crowds dwindle and dissolve, and even the drunks somehow make off. The strip-tease girls in shabby suits, and carrying shabby bags, travel home on the underground, meeting the office cleaners on their way to work. A few whores linger on to pick up stragglers, or just out of restlessness, not wanting to go to bed.

The orchestras are silent at last; doors are shut, lights put out. Fiddlers, ponces, pimps and pandars, like golden youths and girls, home have gone and ta'en their wages. Readers of porno-books, viewers of porno-films, like the strippers who stripped for them – all, all are stretched out, single, or side by side, or clasped together, asleep.

For myself, on the Embankment by Cleopatra's Needle, I watch the Thames flow past; think of its beginnings, a clear, rippling stream, and here a muddy, heavy-moving river, soon to be lost in the ocean. Occasionally a lighted boat glides by, arousing in me a momentary pang. Even now, when the illusion has been so often exploded, I can still imagine that just to be off, to go somewhere else, may bring solace. The delight of going through a door never to be opened again! Of tiptoeing out of a room never to be entered again! Of disengaging from a last embrace! But, of course, other doors will be opened, other rooms entered, other embraces exchanged. The boat going out on the tide in due course comes in on the tide.

Back in my room by the Inner Temple I brace myself for the next edition, listening for the rotary presses, and then for the vans starting up to take it away. Soon the dawn will be breaking round the dome of St Paul's, and I shall be making tea.

'Sleepin' alone tonight, luv?'

'Straight up.
Top floor.
Ten quid.'

A quick one between races at
Wembley Greyhound Stadium

Soho girlie shows are never empty

At the 'Flamingo', a cellar beat club in Gerrard Street.
No lights, no bars, nothing but the big beat.
The cellar is galvanized with a strange excitement,
taken for granted by its inmates.

114

Friday night, the big dance night at the Leicester Square Mecca.
Ultra-violet lights, two bars, two big bands.
It's like being in a 'thirties liner
on the way to dreamland with the band playing
your favourite anniversary waltz in strict tempo.

The T Bones

It's a fine summer night and I'm up
front with 15,000 fans listening to
big beat. For the first time at these
big jazz and blues festivals the pure
jazzmen are outnumbered by the
pop groups. But many of these get
a cool reception because the fans
are mostly for 'trad'. Gary Farr
('magnetic son of Britain's best-ever
heavyweight boxer') sweats blood
to turn the tide.

116

The tide is turned for pop by Ronnie
Jones, an American negro living
and working in Britain, who gives a
memorable performance. After one
number straight, he tears off his
black necktie; he whips the mike
cord about himself like a tame
serpent and frugs ecstatically to the
beat with sweat coursing down his
face. *Everyone* is on his feet,
chanting and swaying.

Sax-player of the Graham Bond Organization

Roger Peacock of the Mark Leeman Five

This is Shoreditch Town Hall, and the atmosphere's very neighbourly.
Lots of big mums and big girls make wrestling seem a homely sport.
At first glance that is. But as buttocks thrash about in frantic combat
screams and insults pierce the flare-lit arena.
I would not like to be a gladiator before *them* on an open verdict.

119

Blues singer Kim Cordell
sings torch 'thirties songs at Dan Farson's Victorianized 'Waterman's Arms'
in Millwall to a mixed audience of Chelsea Mods and locals.

Music Hall emerged from the pubs
of the East End. After years in the
wilderness, it is back there. Dozens
of pubs, such as the 'Black Lion',
the 'City Arms', the 'Iron Bridge',
the 'Pride of the Isle', the 'Rising
Sun' and the 'Waterman's Arms',
vibrate with every kind of music,
mostly with song.

Surrounded by dwarf early Victorian terrace-houses, the 'Pride of the Isle'
on the Isle of Dogs is a beautiful old pub.
It is like a ship inside, with low wooden ceilings and between-the-wars mirrors.
A very young visiting pop group, the Deerstalkers,
plays to the local girls and a covey of Dutch women from a nearby ship.

Dressed up East Enders listen to a resident trio in the 'Boleyn',
a huge Victorian gin palace in the Barking Road, West Ham.

The Beat's Progress: Scene One. London is a great clearing house for thousands of wandering young outcasts. For them, the city is all things. Hitch-hiking beats flock in on Fridays and for the big jazz events: to have a good time, to listen to the music in the clubs and to make new friends. They seldom work, and survive by sleeping around with whoever will give them a shake-down, then moving on. Boy and girl wait for a lift on the North Circular Road, the last lap of the ride to the Big Smoke.

Close up.
The heroine of this drawing is alone and seventeen.
She has left her home in the provinces and is bound for London
on a night train with all she possesses.

Close up.
Ray, occupation folk musician, with admirer. 'Finch's' is strictly Folk or Country and Western. After a while, everybody drifts off to hear a group play in a nearby cellar.

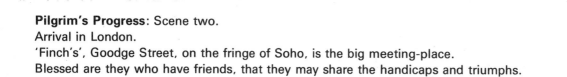

Pilgrim's Progress: Scene two.
Arrival in London.
'Finch's', Goodge Street, on the fringe of Soho, is the big meeting-place.
Blessed are they who have friends, that they may share the handicaps and triumphs.

Rod
Emmett

Pilgrim's Progress: Scene Three.
Country and Western Night at the Ken Colyer Jazz Club, Great Newport Street.
Ray Emmett and Blue Jim play a Bob Dylan number. Folk music is what
is left of romance in these 1960's.

Pilgrim's Progress: Scene Four.
Eleven o'clock;
last drink before closing time at 'Finch's'.

130

Pilgrim's Progress: Scene Five.
One o'clock;
after the Jazz Festival.

'Satire' is on hand at 'The Establishment' in Greek Street, Soho —
'London's First Satirical Night Club'.
The Establishment was founded by Peter Cook to lash corruption in high places,
but the satirists have moved on, and now, under a new regime,
its present clientele listens dutifully to 'satirical' cabaret.
The roulette tables bring in the lolly.

The strip clubs are packed.
Membership is sold at the door,
and the crowds run from caps to
bowlers. Gone are the days of the
bald-headed elderly business-man:
they play for every pocket. This one
is a favourite haunt of sharply
dressed young bachelor industrial
workers. An impeccable Oxbridge
voice introduces the substance of
everyman's sex fantasies.

For this new audience for their trade nubile strippers present in turn:
the new French maid who unexpectedly satisfies your wish with delightful compliance;
a blind date who is more than willing . . .

Only the continued announcement of 'our uncensored and uninhibited film show' elsewhere on the premises relieves the silent tension.

Chelsea:
outside the closed pubs the sports-car set assemble for a party.

MURIEL of the Colony Room

Abide in Me and I in you

My name is Muriel.
I am the Goddess of the Soho Night,
and a friend of artists (especially if
they're well-known). I run a select
private bar called 'The Colony
Room'. A good place to have
several before and after taking the
road to the places that follow.

All-night cafés,
Old Compton Street, Soho.

Waiting for the action

'The Ace Cafe',
on the North Circular Road;
G.H.Q. of the Rockers, the ton-up boys or leather boys. Grimly 'thirties transport in
style, the 'Ace' is used by truck-drivers and bewildered strangers during the week.
But at the week-end, on Friday and Saturday nights, it changes into an offbeat
niterie packed with Rockers and their girls. No one dances or stays very long;
maybe a fast coke, then off on the motor-bikes to roar up and down the luridly-lit
highway.

'The Savage Eye': Lesbos in Chelsea

'Cowboy' and 'Tom the Pill' Rockers (slang for a motor-bike) are much tougher and despise Mods as softies and climbers.

Midnight approaches. What
happens after the theatres and
pubs close? Plenty. This isn't 1956!
A medley of crowded cafés, gaming
clubs, drinking dens, swinging
discotheques and costly cabarets
are able to keep an army of rakes
on the go-go till dawn's early light.

The Royal Opera House, Covent Garden.
The show is over, and the first sacks of potatoes
have already arrived in the nearby market.

Supper in the Edwardian comfort of Rules, Maiden Lane.

Rake's Progress Scene 1.
At Annabel's, the OK establishment discothèque,
the toffs get in on the big beat too.

Rake's Progress Scene 2.
London's fame as a gambling centre
in William Hogarth's day has now
been restored. Gaming is legal
again. In a good week, says the
Sunday Times, the London clubs
alone have a turnover of ten million
pounds and at Aspinall's rakes are
to be seen again, caught up in the
seductive timelessness of a
demonic urge that finds little out-
ward expression.

Night turns to morning, and
London's daily cycle starts again. . .